D0018677

TWISTED TRUE TALES FROM SCIENCE

DISASTER DISCOVERIES

STEPHANIE BEARCE

WITH ILLUSTRATIONS BY
ELIZA BOLLI

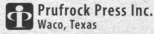
Prufrock Press Inc.
Waco, Texas

Library of Congress Cataloging-in-Publication Data

Names: Bearce, Stephanie, author.
Title: Twisted true tales from science : disaster discoveries / by Stephanie
  Bearce.
Other titles: Disaster discoveries
Description: Waco, Texas : Prufrock Press Inc., [2017] | Audience: Ages 9-12.
  | Includes bibliographical references.
Identifiers: LCCN 2016051029 | ISBN 9781618215741 (pbk.)
Subjects: LCSH: Natural disasters--Juvenile literature. | Disasters--Juvenile
  literature. | Industrial accidents--Juvenile literature.
Classification: LCC GB5019 .B43 2017 | DDC 363.34--dc23
LC record available at https://lccn.loc.gov/2016051029

Prufrock Press Inc.
P.O. Box 8813
Waco, TX 76714-8813
Phone: (800) 998-2208
Fax: (800) 240-0333
http://www.prufrock.com

TABLE OF *Contents*

IT'S EARTH'S FAULT

HUMANS CAUSED IT

DISASTER DAREDEVILS

IT'S EARTH'S FAULT

VESUVIUS

The morning of August 24, 79 A.D. was sunny and warm. Seventeen-year-old Pliny the Younger spent the morning as he usually did, studying the lessons assigned by his uncle and tutors and writing letters. His uncle, Pliny the Elder, was an official in the Roman court and in charge of the Roman fleet in the bay of Naples. They lived in the town of Misenum.

The residents of Misenum were relieved that the day was calm. There had been several ground tremors during the past weeks, shaking buildings and frightening children and animals. But this was a nice normal summer day with shopping at the market and work in the fields and on the docks.

After a morning full of studies and bookwork, Pliny the Younger and his uncle had both taken time away from the heat of the afternoon to rest inside in the cool shade. It was Pliny the Younger's mother who noticed the strange cloud across the bay.

She roused Pliny the Elder from his afternoon rest and had him look toward Mount Vesuvius. They saw from the window a tall cloud that resembled an umbrella pine with a huge trunk and swirls of smoke that spread like branches high above.

They saw from the window a tall cloud that resembled an umbrella pine with a huge trunk and swirls of smoke that spread like branches high above.

Pliny the Elder realized something disastrous had happened across the bay and, as an official of the court, felt it was his duty to investigate. As he was organizing a ship and crew, Pliny the Elder received a message from a friend who was stranded at the base of Mount Vesuvius. Pliny knew that he was mounting a rescue mission. Disaster of some sort had hit Herculaneum and Pompeii. If he could get his ship in to shore, he would haul out as many people as he could.

With a warning to Pliny the Younger to stay home and guard his mother, Pliny the Elder left for his voyage across the bay. As his boat came close to the mountain, small pumice stones began to rain down on the ship and a dusting of ash fell. The crew could see fires burning up and down the mountain. Some of the blazes were 100 feet high.

Pliny was able to land his ship and find his friend. He spent the night in the home of his friend, debating about what they should do next. They hoped that when morning arrived the skies would clear and they would be able to make their way back across the bay to the safety of Misenum. But when morning should have come, the sky was still dark and gray as night.

Pumice stones were falling more frequently and the showers of ash were more intense. The people strapped pillows on their heads to protect themselves from the falling stones and made their way to the shore. But the sea had become wild

> The people strapped pillows on their heads to protect themselves from the falling stones and made their way to the shore.

with waves. There was no way Pliny could launch his boat. The ash became thicker and fell like a blizzard. With his nostrils and lungs filled with poisonous gas and ash, Pliny the Elder died on the shore.

In the cities of Pompeii and Herculaneum, the ash fell in layers more than 9 feet deep. It buried everything in an almost concrete-like formation that preserved casts of the victims' bodies and the cities' buildings.

Those who escaped told harrowing tales of animals and people dying from poisonous gasses and of fires that raged up and down the mountain. They saw the water sucked out of the bay of Naples only to rush back in and flood the ports and docks. People who had escaped the burning rocks and gasses drowned in the tsunami.

Friends of Pliny the Elder made it back to Misenum and told of his death. It was Pliny the Younger who wrote down all that he heard from witnesses and sent the information in two letters to the historian Tacitus. These two letters were the only written accounts of the devastation of the eruption of Mount Vesuvius. It claimed the

[They not only found intact streets and buildings, but also discovered strange voids in the ground—holes where there was no ash or dirt.]

lives of more than 1,000 people and obliterated two towns from the face of the Earth. For many years, people remembered the volcanic eruption of Mount Vesuvius, but after a few generations the history was forgotten.

Herculaneum was rediscovered in 1738 when workmen were digging a foundation for a summer palace for the King of Naples. Workmen literally struck "pay dirt" when they found perfectly preserved artwork and jewelry. A few years later, the

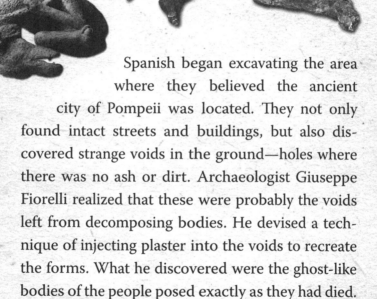

Plaster casts of three victims killed by the eruption of Mount Vesuvius

Spanish began excavating the area where they believed the ancient city of Pompeii was located. They not only found intact streets and buildings, but also discovered strange voids in the ground—holes where there was no ash or dirt. Archaeologist Giuseppe Fiorelli realized that these were probably the voids left from decomposing bodies. He devised a technique of injecting plaster into the voids to recreate the forms. What he discovered were the ghost-like bodies of the people posed exactly as they had died. Some of the plaster casts are so detailed that the eyelashes are visible on the bodies.

By 1760, it was fashionable to tour the ancient city of Pompeii and view the preserved buildings, body casts, and artifacts from the ancient city. Any wealthy person who was going on a grand tour of Europe had to stop at Pompeii. The fascination with the ancient disaster still haunts the city, as nearly 3 million tourists view the city each year.

Scientists and researchers are still excavating the ruins at both Pompeii and Herculaneum and have discovered that the people who lived in both cities were extremely healthy. Even the skeletons of servants show them to be well nourished with nearly perfect teeth. The cities had well-developed sewer and water systems with indoor plumbing and high standards of hygiene. Because the ash killed the people and covered the city at the same time, these are some of the most well-preserved ruins in the world. What was a disaster thousands of years ago has become a historical window into the ancient Roman world.

ALEPPO QUAKES

In 1138, the City of Aleppo was a bustling metropolis with thousands of people living in the city trading goods like spices, cloth, and jewelry. The Middle Eastern city saw traders arrive in camel caravans and crusaders come on horses from Europe. It boasted modern stone buildings and even had a castle complete with turrets. It was the pride of its citizens and a place where Muslims, Christians, and Jewish people lived and worked together.

But in October of that year, the ground of the mighty city started shaking. Ibn al-Qalanisi, a writer of that time who lived in Damascus, recorded feeling a

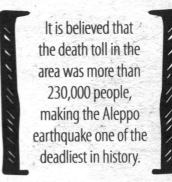

It is believed that the death toll in the area was more than 230,000 people, making the Aleppo earthquake one of the deadliest in history.

small quake on October 10 and then a big quake on October 11. Damascus is 224 miles from the town of Aleppo, and yet the earthquake was strong enough to shake the buildings there.

The quake caused Aleppo's city walls to crumble and buildings to crash. The beautiful castle was destroyed and 600 guards were killed when it fell.

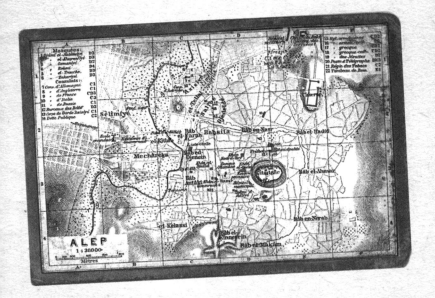

The church fell in on itself, and mosques and temples collapsed. Survivors fled to nearby cities, telling of horrible destruction and death.

It is believed that the death toll in the area was more than 230,000 people, making the Aleppo earthquake one of the deadliest in history. Amazingly the people of Aleppo returned and rebuilt their city. Today it is sometimes called Halab and is located in the country of Syria.

MYSTERY FLOOD

It was a mystery in 1607 and is still a mystery today. What caused the flood at England's Burnham-on-Sea?

It was a sunny day in January with no signs of foul weather. Local farmers were tending to their livestock, and housewives were cooking over their fires. There was no clue that in moments a wall of water would come rushing into the Bristol Channel.

But at 9 a.m. a huge wave of water broke the sea wall and flooded the villages and farmland. Farmers were

> But at 9 a.m. a huge wave of water broke the sea wall and flooded the villages and farmland. Farmers were swept out to sea with their cattle, goats, and pigs.

swept out to sea with their cattle, goats, and pigs. Whole families were washed away along with their homes. Thirty villages in the area were flooded with water 12 feet deep, and more than 2,000 people were killed.

Stories were told of people grabbing on to trees to save themselves or putting children up in the rafters in hopes they would survive. One baby actually washed up out of the flood waters in its wooden cradle being guarded by a pet cat. But

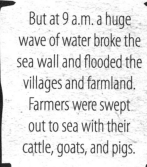

more often there were stories of mothers who had their children swept out of their arms, and family members who were never seen again.

For centuries, it was thought that the breakdown of the sea wall was caused by a storm surge out at sea. Many people living in the 1600s believed it was a warning from God that they needed to reform or face the judgment of God with another great flood. Pamphlets were printed that told people to beware the judgment of God.

But now scientists are questioning whether it was actually a flood. Maybe it was a tsunami. Some eye-witness reports of the time tell of the sea floor being exposed just before the flood. This is one of the signs of a tsunami. Geologists have also found a thick layer of seashells and ocean debris that indicate the force of a tidal tsunami deposit.

Other evidence cited by researchers is the speed at which the flood came. There was no warning with slowly rising water—it seemed to be an immediate event with water rushing in and then pulling people and objects back into the ocean.

> Stories were told of people grabbing on to trees to save themselves or putting children up in the rafters in hopes they would survive.

But if it was a tsunami, what caused it? There was no record of an earthquake in the region. Could it have been a landslide off the continental shelf of the ocean? Or perhaps it was caused by a combination of small earthquake and underwater shelf slide. Nobody knows for sure. The 1607 disaster remains a mystery that scientists are determined to solve—a discovery still yet to come.

1816—THE YEAR WITHOUT A SUMMER

It was the strangest weather people had ever seen. In the Alps of Switzerland, people thought the world was coming to an end when bloodred snow covered the ground. Other parts of Europe reported orange sunsets that kept glowing in the sky long after the sun had set.

In New England, summer never came. Frost stayed on the ground in April and ice filled the rivers in May. A snowstorm hit New York City on June 6 and 7, dropping half a foot of snow when New Yorkers were ready to see tulips and green grass.

And it didn't get better. It was so cold on the Fourth of July that farmers had to break the ice to give their livestock fresh water. Independence Day celebrations were held inside near a fireplace so people could keep warm.

Crops around the Northern Hemisphere were killed. Potato crops in Ireland failed. In China, the rice wouldn't grow, and people were so hungry they ate dirt. Fruit trees were frozen, and oats never sprouted. In a world that survived on the produce of local farms, it meant

> A snowstorm hit New York City on June 6 and 7, dropping half a foot of snow when New Yorkers were ready to see tulips and green grass.

starvation and death. Nearly 90,000 people died from disease and starvation.

Nobody understood what had caused the strange weather. Some people believed God was angry at the world and conducted prayer meetings and revivals. Others were sure it was the work of the devil and speculated that it was caused by witchcraft. Some scientists believed it was a shift in the magnetism of the Earth, and still others thought it might be the fault of sunspots.

None of these ideas were correct, but in a world without radios, telephones, televisions, or even telegraphs, there was no way that people could know the strange weather was caused by a volcano that had erupted thousands of miles away the year before.

[
The top of the ancient volcano blew off, spewing tons of ash and rocks into the air.
]

In the spring of 1815, on the quiet island of Sumbawa, Indonesia, an old mountain started rumbling. Villagers had felt earthquakes and rumblings before, but nothing serious had ever happened. Many thought it was the anger of the gods shaking the land. But in April, Mount Tambora literally exploded.

The top of the ancient volcano blew off, spewing tons of ash and rocks into the air. The explosion was so huge that soldiers on the island of Java 780 miles away thought someone had fired a cannon. They were sure that the island was being attacked and sent scouts out to search, but they didn't find any invading armies. Instead they began seeing clouds of dust roll through the skies.

More eruptions followed the first. Columns of fire shot into the air, and rocks rained down on the island. Then volcanic ash rained down from the sky, piling up to more than 3 feet deep. The weight of the ash collapsed roofs and killed those who were inside. It is estimated that more than 10,000 people were killed directly by the volcanic eruption. Still more died because the ash killed the crops and left people to starve.

The explosion took off a third of the mountain. It left a crater 4 miles wide and more than 3,000 feet deep. It was the largest volcanic explosion ever recorded in human history.

The volcano ejected 200 million tons of sulfur dioxide into the stratosphere. Jet streams carried the sulfur dioxide to the Northern Hemisphere. By the spring of 1816, people in Europe, China, and North America could see a strange haze in the sky. It was the sulfur dioxide reflecting the sun's light away from the Earth, making the temperature on Earth cooler. It also caused fog, huge rain clouds, snow, and floods. It took nearly 3 years for the sulfur dioxide to be pulled out of the atmosphere by gravity.

HOW BIG WAS THE EXPLOSION?

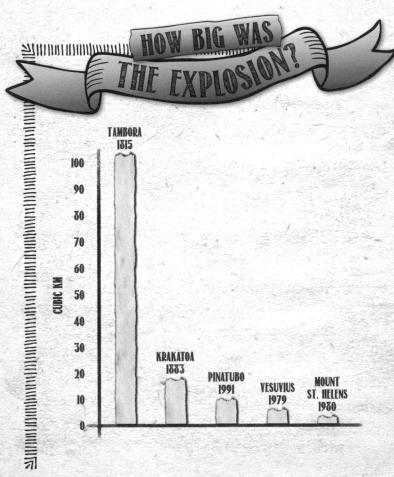

SUPER SOLAR STORM

On September 1, 1859, British scientist Richard Carrington went to work in his private observatory just as he did every morning. His current project was recording the strange sunspots that covered the face of the sun. Scientists knew that the spots changed and moved, but they were not sure what the spots did. Were they firestorms swirling around the sun? Cold spots? Magnetic storms? Could the spots have any effect on the Earth's weather or climate? Carrington hoped his observations would answer some of those questions.

That morning he was doing his usual work, drawing the sunspots he saw projected onto a screen. Then suddenly, two brilliant beads of blinding white light appeared over the sunspots. He observed the phenomena for 5 minutes as the bright light contracted and finally disappeared. What had he seen? Carrington

Richard Carrington

was mystified, but he dutifully recorded the incident. Surely he would learn the answer someday.

That night, the midnight skies came alive with blazing red and orange lights. The sky was so bright that workers got out of bed thinking that it was morning. Birds began singing, fooled into thinking the sun had risen. And around the globe, telegraph operators found the telegraph lines failing or, worse, spewing sparks and electric shocks. In 1859, the telephone had not been invented, and the telegraph was the way the world communicated.

By 8 a.m. on September 2, telegraph operators in North America knew something very strange was going on. Many of them found that their machines would not work when plugged in to their batteries. But if they unplugged them, they could transmit messages every 30 to 90 seconds using the electricity in the air.

Some telegraph operators reported being shocked by their machines. One operator was shocked so hard it knocked him out. Other operators saw sparks fly out of their machines and set papers on fire.

At Kew Gardens, a set of magnetometers went wild. They had been set up by scientists to study the Earth's magnetic field. That morning, the meter recordings were literally off the charts. Scientists were baffled.

Then there were the reports of the Aurora Borealis, the Northern Lights. This light display dipped so far south that people in Cuba and Hawaii reported seeing the night sky turn purple, green, red, and orange.

Over the next few days, the skies returned to normal and the telegraphs started working correctly. Everyday citizens chalked it up to strange weather patterns. But scientists, like Carrington, believed that this was evidence that the sun had bursts of electrical energy that could affect the Earth. What they didn't realize at the time was that they had just witnessed one of the largest solar flares in recorded history.

Today, scientists refer to this solar storm as the Carrington Event. Carrington's observations helped astronomers realize that there are storms on the surface of the sun and solar flares that explode and that these can affect the climate and weather

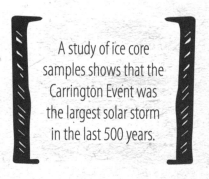

A study of ice core samples shows that the Carrington Event was the largest solar storm in the last 500 years.

on Earth. Solar flares cause huge fluctuations in the Earth's magnetic field. A study of ice core samples shows that the Carrington Event was the largest solar storm in the last 500 years. Scientists also know that solar storms are like a hurricane cycle and go through calm periods and then escalate into high intensity. It is very possible that there may be another storm just as large as the Carrington event. But at least now scientists will know what is happening and may be able to warn the world.

SOLAR DISASTER

Cell phones, satellite communications, television, computer cloud storage—the world has become more complex since 1859. What would happen if a solar flare the size of the Carrington Event hit Earth now? Catastrophe.

It would knock out communications around the world. GPS would stop working. It could damage the International Space Station. Both cell phones and landline telephones would be affected, and emergency services would be unavailable. It could fry electrical lines, explode transformers, and shut down electrical generators. The world would go dark.

That is why NASA and space agencies worldwide place a high priority on watching and predicting solar flares. Emergency plans are in place to shut down satellites, electrical grids, and generators if a solar flare is predicted.

TRI-STATE TERROR

March 18, 1925 was an exceptionally warm day for so early in the spring. Students in De Soto, IL, were enjoying afternoon recess, playing tag and running around the schoolyard. Seven-year-old Betty Moroni ran outside to join the other children for recess, but it was so windy she could barely stand up. Her brother and some of the older boys threw their caps in the air to see how far they would fly.

The teacher came outside, looked at the clouds swirling overhead, and called the children back inside. Trooping back in, Moroni sat down next to her 10-year-old sister. The teacher asked the boys to close the window because it looked like it was going to storm. The next thing Moroni knew, windows were popping and glass was spraying around the room. Wind as loud and strong as a freight train twisted around the schoolhouse and collapsed the walls.

> Wind as loud and strong as a freight train twisted around the schoolhouse and collapsed the walls.

Moroni remembers waking up and crawling through broken timber, smashed glass, and jagged nails to get out of the schoolhouse. Dazed and confused, she found a man who helped her walk to the site where her house used to be. But the house was in ruins. Her mother and father and two little sisters were there, but her brother and two older sisters were missing.

Hours later, they learned that her two older sisters had died in what was later called the Tri-State Tornado. It ripped through Missouri, Indiana, and

Illinois and destroyed 15,000 homes. It killed nearly 700 people and still holds the record for the longest and deadliest tornado in history. Moroni spent the rest of her long life afraid of severe storms.

One of the reasons so many people died in the 1925 Tri-State Tornado was because there was no severe weather warning system. Radios had only been broadcasting for a few years, and there was no regular daily forecast of the weather and no way to warn people when severe weather was on its way.

People living in the middle of the United States knew about tornadoes, but they didn't know the warning signs or what to look for. They also did not know that they needed to get underground to survive a tornado. It was after this huge disaster that scientists began researching ways to help people survive these violent storms.

Research done by the National Weather Service shows that the Southern Plains Area of the central United States has more tornadoes on average than any other part of the world. The wide open plains are conducive to tornado creation because cold, dry air coming from the Rocky Mountains often collides with the warm, wet air of the rivers and grasslands of the region. When these two air masses meet, they provide the right ingredients for making a tornado.

Tornadoes are violent rotating columns of air that come from the base of a thunderstorm and reach down to Earth. Tornadoes can have winds that blow from 110 miles per hour to more than 300

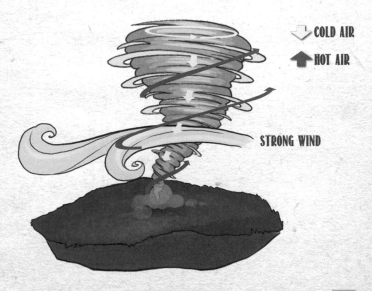

COLD AIR

HOT AIR

STRONG WIND

mph. They can stay on the ground for as little as 5 minutes or, as in the Tri-State Tornado, as long as 3 hours. Each year, there are about a thousand tornadoes that touch down in the United States. That's more than any other country in the world.

> Tornadoes can have winds that blow from 110 miles per hour to more than 300 mph. They can stay on the ground for as little as 5 minutes or, as in the Tri-State Tornado, as long as 3 hours.

Today there are early warning systems that can tell people to take cover when a tornado is approaching. Most towns and cities have tornado sirens to give citizens notice to take cover. Radios and televisions broadcast warnings, schools practice tornado drills so students will be protected in case of a storm, and many homes, especially in that area of the U.S., have tornado shelters.

TWISTER TRUTH

Texas is the tornado champion. It gets hit with an average of 125 tornadoes every year. Oklahoma comes in second place with 57, while Kansas and Florida tie for third with 55 tornadoes each year.

The city that wins for most tornado hits is Oklahoma City. They've been keeping track since 1893, and since then, they have been hit by more than 100 tornadoes. Second place goes to Huntsville, AL.

The winds in tornadoes can cause damage that seems to defy the laws of physics. After a tornado, people often report seeing pieces of straw or hay sticking out of wood like a porcupine. In 2015, a tornado in Pampa, TX, sucked corn stalks out of the field and threw them up in the atmosphere so high they became coated with ice. Then the ice-covered stalks rained back down, creating corn stalk hail. And in 1943, a farmer in Michigan reported that a tornado took all the feathers off 30 of his chickens. The chickens lived through the windy plucking.

THE TUNGUSKA EVENT

More than 100 years ago, a fireball appeared in the sky above Siberia and a huge explosion rocked the Earth, destroying 830 square miles of forest. But what was it that caused so much devastation? Was it a comet or meteor crashing through Earth's atmosphere? Or was it something more exotic, like a small black hole colliding with Earth? Maybe it was an extraterrestrial space vehicle blowing up in the stratosphere?

Scientists are still arguing about exactly what caused the Tunguska Event, mainly because the cataclysmic event wasn't investigated until 19 years after it happened.

Siberia has always been a remote and difficult place to travel. Winter is brutally cold, with winter temperatures dropping to -30 degrees Fahrenheit. In the summer thaw, the ground turns into a mushy mess that makes travel very difficult.

Scientist Leonid Kulik had read reports of the strange explosion that happened in 1908. Newspaper stories said that one man was sitting

Leonid Kulik, 1929

on the front porch of the Vanavara Trading Post when he saw the sky split in two and a great fireball descend. Seconds later, he was thrown from his chair by a heat blast so strong it felt like his shirt was on fire. The man was 40 miles from the actual explosion site.

In 1921, Kulik was the curator of the meteorite collection at the St. Petersburg museum. When he read the old reports of the Tunguska event, he was sure it must have been a meteorite that entered Earth's atmosphere. Here was a golden opportunity to add to the museum's collection and do some research. He put a team together and tried to reach the site, but the weather was so bad they gave up without ever finding the crash site.

Six years later, Kulik had raised enough money to put together another research team, and in the summer of 1927, they found the impact site. But it was not what anyone expected. It was much worse.

A huge forest still lay in ruins. Eighty million trees were still lying on the ground in a radial pattern with their roots ripped from the earth. As the team traveled to the center of the impact site, there were upright trees, but they had been stripped of

all their branches and bark. It looked like a forest of telephone poles.

Kulik's team got to work, determined to find the meteor that had caused this devastation. Surely there would be a large piece of rock to bring back to the museum. But after weeks of searching, they never found a single large crater. They did find

> Eighty million trees were still lying on the ground in a radial pattern with their roots ripped from the earth.

some smaller craters, but there were no meteoritic rocks—no evidence of any meteor. Puzzled, the team left the area.

When Kulik wrote up his scientific report, he made a hypothesis that the meteor had exploded in the atmosphere. That would explain the ball of fire people had seen and the damage to the forest. The fragments of the meteor would have vaporized or could have been small and sank in the swampy ground. Most scientists agreed with Kulik's ideas. And in 1934, Soviet scientists suggested that it might have been an icy comet that exploded, and that was why there was no trace of meteoritic rock.

But with no absolute conclusions, it has left room for some wild speculations about alternative scenarios. In 1973, American physicists published an article that suggested a small black hole had collided with Earth and there had been a matter-antimatter explosion. And a German scientist has proposed that it was an explosion of underground magma gas. And, of course, some amateur UFO enthusiasts still think it was the explosion of an extraterrestrial spaceship.

Although scientists can't say for sure what caused the Tunguska explosion, they are pretty sure it was either a comet or a meteor exploding in the atmosphere, as Kulik suggested. Of course, that leaves scientists wondering and searching the skies for the next time a piece of space ice or rock will cause an explosion on Earth.

THE EXPLODING LAKE

The villagers of Lake Nyos, Cameroon, tell of an ancient legend—a story of dead people and evil spirits who live in the depths of lakes. Sometimes the spirits get angry with the villagers and rise up from the waters. They kill all the people and their animals. Then they go back into the lake and rest. Until the next time the villagers do something wrong—then the spirits will kill again.

In 1986, most people thought the lake legends were just old ghost stories—something uncles told at night to make children shriek. People had been living near the lake for hundreds of years, herding cattle and farming small plots of land. They had never seen any ghosts, and the lake was used for fishing.

On the evening of August 21, Ephriam Che was getting ready for bed when he heard a rumbling sound. He stepped outside his mud-brick house, looked down into the valley below, and saw the moon shining on Lake Nyos. It looked peaceful. Then he noticed a mist rising from the lake. He figured it must mean rain was coming. He told his wife and children goodnight and went to bed because he didn't feel well.

> When Che entered the small compound of thatched huts, he found all of Suley's family dead in their beds.

In the morning, Che got up and went about the normal morning chores. He headed down the side of the mountain to the lake below. Partway down the hill, he was met by one of his neighbors, Halima Suley. She was frantic. Something was wrong with her whole family.

Che went with her to see if he could help. When Che entered the small compound of thatched huts, he found all of Suley's family dead in their beds. Her father, her children, her aunts and uncles. All 31 of her family members were dead.

Then Che noticed the strange silence. There were no birds singing. No insects buzzing. No cows bellowing. They were all dead, too.

Terrified, Che ran down the hill and into the village. He ran from hut to hut, and in each one he found the same thing: The bodies of his friends and family. Some died in their beds. Others seemed to have collapsed near cooking fires or in doorways. The spirits of the lake had killed them all.

Nearly 1,800 people died that night. Almost everyone living in a 15-mile radius was found dead near their homes or in their beds. More than 3,500 head of livestock were dead in the fields, along with hundreds of birds, small mammals, reptiles, and insects. And the water in Lake Nyos had turned from beautiful blue to ugly red.

No one understood what had happened, and because of the remote location of Lake Nyos, it took several days for word of the catastrophe to reach the rest of the world. As soon as the scientific community learned about the tragedy, they sent experts in to investigate. Had the dormant volcano under the lake suddenly started giving off deadly gasses? Was there going to be a volcanic eruption? Was it safe to go near the lake?

> When the scientists began testing the water they found something very strange. The water of Lake Nyos was full of carbon dioxide.

When the scientists began testing the water, they found something very strange. The water of Lake Nyos was full of carbon dioxide. This is the gas that humans naturally expel from their lungs. It is a by-product of respiration. But it is also known as an *asphyxiant*, a chemical that bonds with your blood in place of oxygen. Breathing in too much carbon dioxide can kill you. And that's what happened at Lake Nyos.

Scientists discovered that deep below the lake is a pocket of magma that leaks carbon dioxide into the floor of the lake. This happens in many crater lakes, but it is not a problem because the waters of the lake circulate and the carbon dioxide releases harmlessly into the air.

But Lake Nyos is unusually still, so the gas builds up in the water in such high concentrations that, if it is released, it will kill anything that breathes oxygen. A release of the carbon dioxide could be caused by a landslide, a volcanic eruption, an earthquake, or even something as simple as a heavy rain disturbing the lake and causing the waters to mix.

After investigating the lake and talking with survivors, scientists believe that on the night of August 21, 1986, something caused 300,000 tons of carbon dioxide to explode from the lake. It formed a gas cloud and drifted into the valley. Because carbon dioxide is heavier than oxygen, the gas cloud hugged the ground. The people in the valley breathed in pure carbon dioxide and suffocated from lack of oxygen.

Families who lived up the mountain away from the valley were not affected because the heavy cloud did not rise that high. That was how Che and his family escaped. A few others, like Suley, passed out from the carbon dioxide but survived. In the whole village of Lake Nyos, there were less than 10 people who lived.

After investigating the lake and talking with survivors, scientists believe that on the night of August 21, 1986, something caused 300,000 tons of carbon dioxide to explode from the lake.

To prevent this type of tragedy from happening again, scientists installed a pump system to cause controlled releases of the carbon dioxide. By doing this, it should not build up to a critical mass and cause another explosion.

Today, people have moved back into the region, and there are now cattle grazing in the fields and villagers growing vegetables. But the people there wonder about the old story of the evil spirit of the lake. Was it really just a ghost story or was it the distant memory of something that happened generations ago? Maybe the explosion in 1986 was not the first, but hopefully it will be the last.

MORE KILLER LAKES?

So far, scientists have only discovered three lakes that can kill with carbon dioxide explosions, and all of them are in Africa. One of these is Lake Monoun, and it is only 60 miles from Lake Nyos. The other is Lake Kivu in the Democratic Republic of Congo.

Just 2 years before the catastrophic explosion at Nyos, 37 people were found dead near Lake Monoun. Investigators were mystified. The dead people showed no signs of poisoning. They thought it might be a chemical attack by terrorists. It wasn't until the Lake Nyos explosion that scientists understood what killed the people at Monoun. Now all three lakes have degassing pumps to keep the villagers safe.

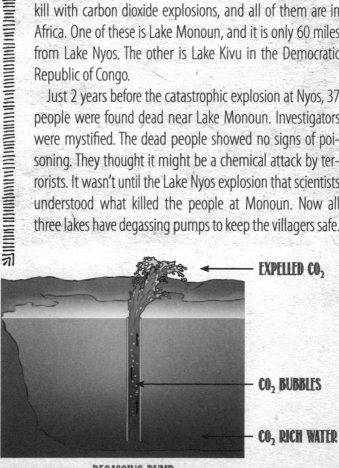

EXPELLED CO_2

CO_2 BUBBLES

CO_2 RICH WATER

DEGASSING PUMP

KILLER TSUNAMI

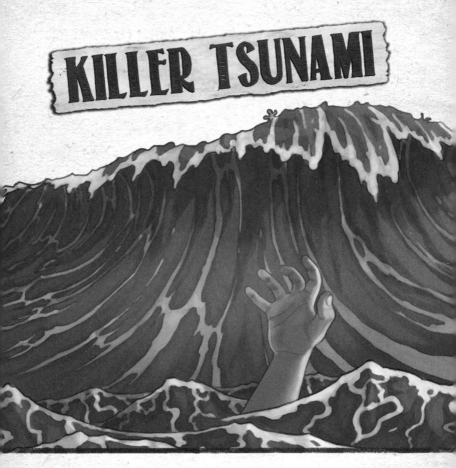

It was a beautiful day on the beaches of Thailand—turquoise water glistened in the sun, and children dug in the golden sand with plastic shovels and pails. Parents unpacked sandwiches and treats for the beach. They laughed and exchanged holiday greetings.

"Happy Boxing Day."

"Did you have a nice Christmas?"

"How was your Hanukkah?"

Hotel workers served drinks and cleaned rooms. They looked forward to being able to spend their time off with family and friends, ringing out the year 2004 and celebrating the new year of 2005. It was a normal holiday season.

But far out in the Indian Ocean, the tectonic plates were moving. The India plate was pushing against the Burma plate as it

> Buzzers went off at the Pacific Tsunami Warning Center in Hawaii. It was an earthquake with a magnitude of 8.5. The worst earthquakes are level 9.0 and above.

had for thousands of years. But on December 26, 2004, the plates ruptured, causing a rip in the ocean floor more than 600 miles long. Rocks, boulders, and ocean floor burst up as a massive earthquake shook the ground.

Buzzers went off at the Pacific Tsunami Warning Center in Hawaii. It was an earthquake with a magnitude of 8.5. The worst earthquakes are level 9.0 and above. This was a gigantic earthquake right in the middle of the Indian Ocean. Scientists conferred. Would this cause a tsunami, a huge tidal wave? They couldn't be sure. It was so far out in the

ocean. Maybe it would never affect the shoreline. But if it did—people should be warned. But there was no warning system—no way to tell the people that giant waves might be headed their way.

On the beach, families stared at the ocean. The water had suddenly left the shore. Wide expanses of rocks and sand that had been covered with ocean were now bare and exposed. Seashells and starfish attracted the attention of some. Others stared out at the horizon. Where had the ocean gone?

Then, on the horizon they heard a noise like thunder. Huge white waves rolled toward the shore—moving faster than anyone could run. People screamed.

"Run! Run!"

Parents grabbed children. Families ran back to

their hotels, back to the town. But the waves were faster. The waves caught everything in their path and pulled both humans and buildings out to sea—swishing and swirling like a giant washing machine.

Some people were pushed up and were able to gasp for air. They clung to logs, beach coolers, mattresses—anything that would float.

Other people felt the ocean pull them under, holding them until there was no oxygen left in their lungs. Their lifeless bodies floated out to sea or washed up on the shore.

The ocean spit some people out miles from the beach—their clothes ripped from their bodies, their bones broken, cut and bleeding but alive. They were the lucky ones. Hundreds, thousands, of others died in the vicious ocean waves.

It became known as the deadliest tsunami in history. More than 230,000 people in 11 countries were killed. It destroyed entire villages, wiped out forests, and left people stunned at the forces of nature.

News of the tsunami spread quickly, and help

poured in from around the world. Medical teams from America, Australia, Canada, Europe, and Asia gave help to the survivors. And teams of scientists got busy trying to figure out how such a disaster could be prevented in the future.

After several years of investigation, a team of scientists came up with a system of measuring rapid changes in sea levels. Special buoys are designed to be placed in the ocean to measure sensitive areas and transmit information in real time to scientists. It is important that the information be immediate, because seconds count in warning for a tsunami. There are now 60 of these buoys deployed world-wide. When the 2004 tsunami hit, there were only six.

In 2004, 90% of the people in the affected area of the Thailand tsunami were killed. In comparison, when the Tōhoku tsunami struck Japan in 2011, only 10% of the people in the affected area died.

This was due to the advancements in the worldwide warning system.

Scientists say there are still improvements to be made. They would like to capture more data to improve their mathematical models, and they still need to learn about how earthquakes close to shore affect the ocean. There is much to be studied. But they hope the warning system they have developed will prevent another tragedy like the tsunami of 2004.

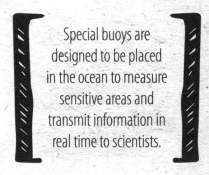

Special buoys are designed to be placed in the ocean to measure sensitive areas and transmit information in real time to scientists.

ANGEL OF THE BEACH

Tilly Smith was 10 years old when the tsunami hit the beach at Phuket, Thailand. She was on vacation with her family, enjoying a walk along the shore, when Smith noticed that the water was strangely frothy. It reminded her of a lesson her teacher had just taught on tsunamis.

She watched the water and realized that it wasn't moving out, but was just coming in toward the shore. Smith became convinced there was going to be a tsunami and tried to warn her parents. But her mother and father didn't believe her.

But Smith didn't give up. She kept insisting that she knew what she was talking about and that her family needed to get off the beach. Smith's little sister became frightened and wanted to get off the beach. Her father agreed to go back to the hotel, but Smith's mother wanted to keep walking along the beach.

Thousands of people died that day, but not one guest at the Smith's hotel died. They had an early warning from a 10-year-old girl who paid attention in geography class.

When they got back to the hotel, Smith's father told a security guard about the frothy water and his daughter's fears. The man began yelling at hotel guests to get off the beach. People packed up and headed toward the hotel.

Then they saw the wall of water roaring in from the ocean. Smith's mother also saw the water and was able to run back to the hotel. The whole family went to the second floor of the hotel and watched as the beach was wiped out by the tsunami.

Thousands of people died that day, but not one guest at the Smith's hotel died. They had an early warning from a 10-year-old girl who paid attention in geography class. Many of the hotel guests believed it was a miracle they were saved and started calling Tilly Smith the Angel of the Beach. But Smith says the real hero is her geography teacher, Mr. Kearny. He gave her the knowledge she needed to save herself and those around her.

TILLY'S STORY

You can watch an interview with Tilly Smith at https://www.youtube.com/watch?v=6C3CJX1-d_8&index=2&list=RD6C3CJX1-d_8.

TALLEST TSUNAMI

The Asian tsunami of 2004 was one of the deadliest in the world. Its 100-foot-tall waves killed 230,000 people and destroyed entire villages. But it was not even close to the tallest tsunami on record.

That dubious honor goes to the tsunami that hit Lituya Bay, Alaska, in 1958 with a wave that was 1,720 feet high—more than 10 times the height of the 2004 tsunami.

An earthquake caused a massive avalanche on the northern shore of Lituya Bay, dumping more than 40 million cubic yards of boulders and rubble into the inlet. The force of the rocks hitting the water caused the gigantic wave to wash the entire length of the bay. Trees were snapped off like toothpicks.

One poor fisherman and his son were anchored in the bay when they heard the avalanche. Howard Ulrich threw his 8-year-old son a life preserver and told him to strap it on. He was afraid it would be the last he ever saw of his son.

Ulrich tried to raise the anchor,

> Amazingly, the small boat stayed upright, and they rode the wave in over the shore and back out into the bay.

but there wasn't time. The huge wave came rolling at them and snapped the anchor chain. Amazingly, the small boat stayed upright, and they rode the wave in over the shore and back out into the bay. Both Ulrich and his son survived the tallest tsunami in recorded history.

BIGGEST AND BADDEST EARTHQUAKES

Earthquakes have been around long before man ever walked on the planet. They are a part of what creates the landmasses where humans and many animals live. But they are also dangerous and cause a great deal of death and destruction.

Before the dawn of modern science, people believed that earthquakes were caused by angry gods or were punishment for something people had done wrong. Now scientists understand that while earthquakes can cause devastation, they are a natural part of how the Earth functions.

Modern scientists have developed a way to warn people about coming earthquakes. They have placed seismometers along fault lines and have connected them through computers. When there is movement at the tectonic plates, the meters alert researchers to the impending danger. Japan is one of the most earthquake prone countries in the world, and it has developed a sophisticated system that uses cell phone technology to tell people when there is an earthquake coming—allowing citizens the chance to take cover a few seconds before the quake hits. This warning system has saved thousands of lives.

EARTHQUAKES OF THE HIGHEST MAGNITUDE ON THE RICHTER SCALE

Location/Date	Magnitude	Results
Valdivia, Chile, 1960	9.5	Caused tsunamis as far away as Hawaii, Japan, and the Philippines; because it was in a less populated area, the death estimates range between 1,000–6,000
Prince William Sound, Alaska, 1964	9.2	Massive underwater landslide killed 30 people and wiped out city of Valdez

Location/Date	Magnitude	Results
Indian Ocean, 2004	9.1–9.3	Launched killer tsunamis resulting in more than 230,000 deaths
Tōhoku, Japan, 2011	9.0	Caused tsunamis that damaged nuclear plants, caused nuclear meltdowns, and killed more than 15,000 people
Kamchatka, Soviet Union, 1952	9.0	Epicenter was 81 miles from shore, but caused 50 tsunamis that killed 2,336 villagers

DEADLIEST EARTHQUAKES

Location/Date	Magnitude	Results
Shaanxi, China, 1556	8.0	Landslides wiped out entire villages, killing 830,000
Hebei, China, 1976	7.8	Poorly built buildings collapsed and killed 240,000–500,000
Haiyuan, China, 1920	7.8	Buildings collapsed in heavily populated areas, killing more than 273,000
Antioch, Syria, 526	est. 7.0	Quake started fires, killing 250,000
Indian Ocean, 2004	9.1–9.3	More than 230,000 killed in 11 countries by resulting tsunami

Science Lab

VORTEX IN A BOTTLE

You don't want to build a tornado. It would destroy your house and mess up the whole neighborhood. Your neighbors would get really angry. But you can build a model of a tornado by creating a water vortex in a bottle. It's fun, and it won't blow down your house.

MATERIALS

- » Water
- » Clear plastic water or soda bottle with a lid
- » Glitter
- » Dishwashing liquid

Fill the bottle with water until it is 3/4 full. Then add a few drops of the dish soap. Pour in a teaspoon of glitter. Put the lid on the bottle and seal it tight.

Turn the bottle upside down and hold it by the neck. Spin the bottle in a circular motion. This will start the water vortex. Hold the bottle still. Can you see the vortex spin?

The water is spinning around the center of the vortex due to centripetal force. (It is an inward force that directs an object or fluid like water to the center of its circular path.) Vortexes that are found in nature include tornadoes, hurricanes, and waterspouts.

Science Lab

WHICH WAY THE WIND?

Y ou can learn which way the wind is blowing by making your own weather vane. Farmers used to put weather vanes on the tops of their barns so they could see which way the wind was blowing—they knew that changes in the wind brought changes in weather.

MATERIALS

- » One sharpened pencil with an eraser top
- » Pen
- » One long straight pin
- » Tag board
- » Small corrugated box
- » Mat knife
- » Adult helper
- » Modeling clay
- » Scissors
- » Compass

Draw a 3-inch-long arrow shape on the tag board and cut it out. Place the straight pin through the center of the arrow. Then push the pin holding the arrow into the eraser tip of the pencil. Make sure the arrow turns freely on the pin. This is the weather vane.

Set the pencil and arrow aside. Take your box and turn it upside down. Mark the sides of the box with the pen, labeling it with the correct directions of North, South, East, and West. Have an adult help you use a mat knife to cut a small hole in the center of the bottom of the box (which should now be facing up). Make sure the hole is large enough for the pencil to fit snugly. Put the pencil in the hole and use modeling clay to anchor the pencil so it will not move.

Place the box outside and orient it so that the directions on the box match true North and South. You may need the help of a compass to place it correctly.

Now all you have to do is wait for a breeze to come along. You will be able to tell which way the wind is blowing and when the wind direction changes.

GLADIATOR DISASTER

The ancient Romans were known for their magnificent buildings, especially their coliseums. The huge open-air stadiums provided seating for crowds as large as 50,000 people. Spectators watched violent displays of gladiators sword fighting and prisoners fighting wild animals. They were very bloody but very popular sports, and the coliseums were full for every event.

But in the early years of the first century B.C., an emperor named Tiberius became the ruler of Rome. He hated the blood and death of gladiator fighting and outlawed the sport. For several years, no one could watch bears attack prisoners or soldiers fight to the death. The Roman citizens were outraged. How could the emperor take away their favorite sports? They loved the blood and gore. The citizens protested, and soon Tiberius was so unpopular he feared for his own life. He had no choice but to reinstate the games.

> The instant the ban was lifted, a man named Atilius started building a new stadium in the town of Fidenae, Italy. He knew people were anxious to get back to watching their favorite deadly sport.

The instant the ban was lifted, a man named Atilius started building a new stadium in the town of Fidenae, Italy. He knew people were anxious to get back to watching their favorite deadly sport. He quickly constructed a wooden amphitheater that was to hold an audience of 50,000 people. Most stadiums of the time were built with concrete, stone, or a combination of the two. But Atilius was in a hurry and, besides, wood was so much cheaper. His profits would be so much greater.

As soon as the last peg was hammered into place, Atilius was selling tickets. He had gladiators lined up to fight and Roman citizens lined up to watch. Atilius was going to be a very rich man.

The day of the fight, people crowded into the new stadium. Men, women, and children climbed the board planks, and settled in on the wooden benches. They were ready for a day of bloody battles. But what happened next was bloodier than any gladiator fight.

A cracking sound exploded in the air. Screams and shouts were heard around the stadium, and people began falling to the ground. Logs and boards splintered as the entire stadium broke apart. The walls collapsed both inward and outward. People were buried under tons of logs, boards, and planks.

It was a scene of death and destruction, but it wasn't the gladiators who fought to the death; it was the audience. The collapse killed more than 20,000 people. Thousands more were severely hurt or maimed. As the Roman citizen Tacitus reported, it was "as destructive as a major war and ended in a moment."

People from the town of Fidenae went to work trying to rescue the survivors. As news spread, people from neighboring villages came to give aid. The wounded were taken to local homes and treated with whatever supplies they could find. It took weeks for them to clear out the disaster site and bury all the dead.

In the aftermath, it was discovered that not only had Atilius been cheap and used only wood, but also he had not built a secure foundation. The collapse was an architectural disaster and still holds the record for the worst man-made building disaster in the world. Modern architecture students are taught about the

disaster of Fidenae to warn them not to take shortcuts or use sub-standard materials.

After the disaster, the Roman Senate banned people with a fortune of less than 400,000 sesterces from hosting gladiator shows. They also made requirements that all amphitheaters have solid foundations and mandatory inspections before being allowed to open to the public. And Atilius? He was banished from the Roman Empire.

THE BEER FLOOD

It all started with a vat of beer as tall as a three-story-tall building. In 1814, the London Brewery of Messrs. Henry Meux and Co. produced more than 100,000 barrels of porter every year. They stored the black-colored beer in huge wooden vats that were held together by giant metal hoops. The hoops were so large that a single hoop weighed 700 pounds.

On the afternoon of October 17, employee George Crick went in to check on the latest brew. He noticed that one of the hoops had slipped on one of the huge vats. Crick had seen this happen before and knew that he needed to get someone in to take a look at it. The hoops slipped two or three times a year, and they always called in a repairman to fix it. So Crick did what he was supposed to do and wrote a note to get a repairman out.

> The vat of fermenting beer exploded. The explosion caused a chain reaction, causing other vats to break and burst out the walls of the brewery.

But just minutes after Crick finished writing the letter, he heard an ear-splitting pop. The vat of fermenting beer exploded. The explosion caused a chain reaction, causing other vats to break and burst out the walls of the brewery.

In seconds, the houses near the brewery were flooded with beer. The poverty-stricken households were no match for the deluge of frothy beer. Some people scrambled up on tables, hoping to avoid drowning in the dark liquid. Some houses were swept off their foundations, and others collapsed from the tsunami of beer.

Rescuers had to wade through a waist-deep river of beer to try and pull people out from the wreckage. Sadly, eight women and children drowned in the beer flood. And just 2 days after the catastrophe, a hastily convened jury declared that the brewery was not at fault for their deaths. It was declared an act of God and that the victims had died "casually, accidentally and by misfortune." The brewery never had to pay the victims' families a dime.

Disasters like the beer flood have led to modern practices of factory inspections. Today factory owners are expected to maintain their equipment and pass safety inspection on a regular basis. The science of risk reduction keeps people safe from new disasters like the beer flood.

THE PESHTIGO FIRE

Fires crackled and burned in the Wisconsin woods during the fall of 1871. Farmers and lumber workers had spent days putting out the fires; just when they would think it was over, another spark would send the woods up in flames. Frustrated, the people searched the sky, desperate for rain. Churches held prayer meetings asking for the much-needed moisture, but the only clouds were those that held smoke and cinders.

On Sunday evening, October 8, the citizens of the town of Peshtigo were getting ready for bed when they heard a roaring sound. Looking out their windows, they saw the skies turn a blazing red. The forest that surrounded the lumber town was in flames.

> Looking out their windows, they saw the skies turn a blazing red. The forest that surrounded the lumber town was in flames.

Desperate parents pulled their children from bed and ran to the river in their nightgowns and underclothes. The heat of the fire was already so strong that breathing caused their lungs to burn. Some people fell as they ran—they never made it to the river. Others who lived too far from the water tried hiding in water wells or covering their bodies with wet blankets. Some hid in cellars, hoping they might survive underground.

Horses, cattle, and people all dove into the icy water. Mothers and fathers clutched their children. Infants cried and people screamed in pain as the white-hot fire rained ash and burning embers on their heads. The only way to keep from being

burned was to keep every part of the body wet. The people poured freezing water on their heads.

The fire raged on for an hour and a half. It was too long for many people. They died of hypothermia from exposure to the freezing water. Some died from inhaling too much smoke or poisonous gasses. Soon the river was full of the bobbing bodies of horses, cattle, and humans.

When the flames finally died down, survivors tried to climb out of the river, but found the soil was too hot to touch. They suffered burns simply by touching the ground. They had no choice but to stay in the frigid waters until it cooled.

The night sky was lit with small fires still burning. The screams had quieted down to soft sobs and moans. Finally, at about 3 in the morning, the ground was cool enough to touch. After 5 long hours in the river, survivors crawled onto the burned riverbanks. They had to climb over the dead bodies of their friends and families. In the darkness and confusion, many people were separated from their families and had no idea if anyone they loved had survived.

As dawn came, the people of Peshtigo saw that their entire town had been burned to the ground. All the homes, churches, stores, and even the soil had been charred to ashes. People began searching for their family and friends. They tried to give first aid to the many people who were burned, but there was very little they could do but offer comfort.

> As dawn came, the people of Peshtigo saw that their entire town had been burned to the ground. All the homes, churches, stores, and even the soil had been charred to ashes.

Some of the young men set off walking to get help from the neighboring towns. By noon, wagons started arriving with supplies of food, water, and bandages. The citizens of neighboring Peshtigo Harbor sent wagons loaded with lumber, nails, and tools—supplies for building coffins.

And there were many coffins to build.

Nobody is quite sure how many people died in the Peshtigo fire. Because the temperature of the fire was so high, many of the bodies were completely incinerated and were never recovered or identified. And Peshtigo had many visitors to the town that week. Young men who had come to the town to work at the lumber mills and help on the railroad were not listed as citizens of the town. There was no accurate count of how many itinerant workers died, but there were at least 200 bodies found at the site of the local tavern.

To this day, the Peshtigo fire is the deadliest fire in North America, but most people have never heard of it. That is because the same night Peshtigo burned, a little town called Chicago also had a fire. News of the Great Chicago Fire made headlines across the country and even around the world. It burned 3 square miles of the city and killed 300 people. By contrast, the Peshtigo fire killed at least 1,200 people (many historians place the number at

1,500). The fire consumed more than 1,875 square miles of forest, towns, and farmland—an area twice the size of Rhode Island.

Scientists have never forgotten the Peshtigo fire, however. Many have studied it for years and call it the Peshtigo Paradigm. They believe the unique combination of wind, geography, forest, and cleared settlement land combined to make the perfect firestorm. These conditions were actually studied by the American and British armies during WWII to help them learn how to make effective firebombs.

Conservationists believe that homebuilders should remember Peshtigo and not build too close to natural forests with flammable materials. Humans need to leave space between themselves and areas where fires are a normal part of nature.

THE HALIFAX EXPLOSION

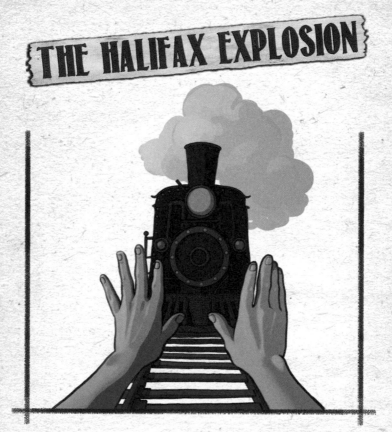

Vince Coleman liked his job as a train dispatcher. He liked the hustle and bustle of the Halifax, Nova Scotia train yard. Out the window of the train station, he could see the Halifax Harbor and watch the ships come and go carrying a number of things. Cargo headed for Europe to help with the Great War effort. Grain and food exported around the world. Halifax was a busy city in 1917, and Coleman was proud of his town and his work.

Telephones had been invented more than 30 years earlier, but they were still con-sidered a luxury. Many businesses had them, but railroads and ships still used the telegraph as their main form of communication. Coleman was busy all day long sending messages to trains throughout Canada and in the Northeastern United States.

The morning of December 6, 1917 was no dif-ferent than any other day for Coleman. He kissed his wife goodbye and headed into work bright and early. There were messages to send and receive. Cargo to move in and out of the railyard and harbor.

> Then a man ran up to Coleman and yelled a warning. The *Mont-Blanc* was full of explosives. The ship was going to explode. Everybody needed to run!

But at 8:45 that morning, Coleman's cowork-ers called to him to come out to the harbor and see what was happening. There, two ships had crashed into each other. One was the *SS Imo*, a Norwegian vessel, and the other was the *SS Mont-Blanc*, a cargo ship from France. The *Imo* did not seem to be seriously damaged and had pulled away from the *Mont-Blanc*, but the other ship was in serious trouble. Flames were spreading across the bow of the ship.

The Norwegian steamship SS Imo

All around the harbor, people stopped their work and stared at the fire, curious about what would happen. Would the new motorized fire truck be called in to help? Would they need to pump water to put out the fire? Schoolchildren crowded at the windows to see what was happening. Men and women gathered on the pier to watch the drama.

Then a man ran up to Coleman and yelled a warning. The *Mont-Blanc* was full of explosives. The ship was going to explode. Everybody needed to run!

Coleman and the other workers started to run, but Coleman stopped himself. If what the man said was true, someone needed to warn the incoming trains. There was a passenger train headed toward the pier. If there was an explosion, all the people on the train would be killed. Coleman ran back to the train office and frantically tapped out a message: "Hold up the train. Ammunition ship afire in harbor making for Pier 6 and will explode. Guess this will be my last message. Good-bye boys."

Seconds later, the harbor exploded in a ball of fire, taking Vince Coleman and 2,000 other people with it.

The Halifax explosion was the largest man-made explosion in the world prior to the atomic bombs dropped on Japan in World War II. *TIME* magazine compared the power of the atomic bomb, Little Boy, to "seven times that of the Halifax explosion."

When the *Mont-Blanc* ship exploded in the Halifax harbor, it obliterated every building within an 800-yard radius. The entire community of

Richmond, Nova Scotia was wiped off the planet.

Nothing was left but broken timbers and scattered bricks. Trees were snapped like matchsticks, and windows shattered in buildings miles away from the blast site. The blast from the explosion pushed the water of the harbor out to sea. As soon as the pressure from the blast dissipated, the water came rushing back into the harbor, creating a tsunami that roared back

The Halifax explosion was the largest man-made explosion in the world prior to the atomic bombs dropped on Japan in World War II.

over the harbor and flooded the railyards and buildings. Wreckage and bodies were washed out to sea.

Fortunately, Coleman's message reached the train station in time. The passenger train was halted and 300 lives were saved. In addition, that message told the world what had happened in Halifax. After the explosion, all communication was cut off. The telegraph and telephone poles were snapped and all communication was down. If Coleman had not gotten that message through, it would have been many hours before the outside world knew what had happened in Halifax. But with Coleman's message, the world pulled together to help the citizens of Halifax. Trains loaded with doctors, nurses, bandages, and medical supplies were sent immediately to Halifax.

The help was welcome, since one of the hospitals was destroyed and there were more than 9,000 people who needed medical treatment. Ships were turned into floating hospitals, and doctors from as far away as Boston began treating children and parents for burns, eye injuries, and broken bones.

Hundreds of people who had been watching the

fire from the windows of their homes, schools, or workplaces were blinded when the blast broke the windows. More than 12,000 buildings were destroyed or severely damaged. Fires broke out throughout the city as wood stoves were overturned and kerosene lanterns set wood structures ablaze. Nine members of the Halifax Fire Department lost their lives that day.

Many of the survivors believed that they had been attacked by German bombs and were terrified that there would be another bombing. Eventually, rescue workers were able to calm those fears and help the injured to understand what had happened.

Because so many had been standing at windows watching the fire, there were more than 5,900 eye injuries reported and 41 people permanently lost their sight. Most of the injuries were caused from the exploding glass. Doctors were called in to help treat the injuries and made extensive studies of the eye injuries. Halifax eventually became known as a premier care center for the blind. A blind relief fund was set up to help care for the victims, and surgery techniques were developed to help preserve as much sight as possible. A school was also established to assist in helping the blind learn new life and work skills.

Although hero Vince Coleman lost his life saving others, his wife and young daughter were injured but survived the blast that day. The dress his daughter wore that day is on display in a Halifax museum. When the town rebuilt, two streets were named after Vince. One street is Coleman Court; the other is Vincent Street.

Vincent Coleman

KILLER FOG

C itizens of London were used to fog. It had been around since the 1800s, when people began heating their homes with coal. When the soot from the coal mixed with the damp London air, it made a dark fog that people said was as thick as "pea soup." The fog had been around for decades, so nobody was all that worried when another "pea souper" rolled in on December 5, 1952.

But this fog was different. It was darker and thicker. By afternoon, the fog was a strange yellow

color that burned the nose and lungs when people breathed. The fog got thicker and darker, until it was so dark that cars couldn't drive during the daytime even using headlights. Drivers gave up and abandoned their cars along the sides of the road. Policemen guided buses through the streets with hurricane lamps and large flashlights. Flights out of London were cancelled and trains stopped running.

For 5 days, the city of London was trapped under a 30-mile-wide cloud of acid smog. Weathermen explained that a high-pressure system had cause a "temperature inversion" that trapped all the coal smoke and kept it from rising or moving out of the area.

Soon people began showing up at London emergency rooms with respiratory infections. Coughing and wheezing, unable to breathe, some of the elderly and infants were so sick they died. Emergency rooms were overwhelmed. Doctors estimated that more than 4,000 people died as a result of breathing the smog.

Officials told parents to keep their children

home from school. Policemen and workers who had to be out in the fog wore facemasks. Even animals were affected. Farmers tied feed sacks soaked in whiskey over the noses of their horses and cows. Many animals died, and when they were autopsied their lungs were black.

The fog eventually lifted on December 9 when a cold wind moved in from the west. The people of London could finally breathe. But politicians and authorities were worried that another killer fog could be just around the corner. They decided that it was important to prevent another disaster and made new laws that encouraged people to stop burning coal and use electricity or natural gas.

It took years for London to make permanent changes, but today homes and businesses use cleaner forms of energy and there is no threat of another killer fog.

THE GREAT MOLASSES FLOOD

In January of 1919, Frank McManus was working as a Boston police officer. It was a warm day for Boston, almost warm enough to want to take your coat off. McManus was enjoying the break from Boston's usual ice and snow.

He strolled over to the call box and picked up the phone, ready to make his noon report. It would be a routine account—nothing out of the usual that morning. Then McManus heard a rat-a-tat-tat sound like a machine gun throwing bullets. He turned around in time to see a five-story metal tank split open and dark thick liquid pour down into the street. He yelled into the phone, "Send all available rescue vehicles and personnel immediately. There's a wave of molasses coming down Commercial Street!"

McManus wasn't kidding. The Purity Distilling Company was in the molasses business in a BIG way. They were storing molasses in the hope of using it to produce liquor. They had filled their five-story-tall metal cylinder with 2.3 million gallons of molasses, but they had never checked on the strength of the tank to hold such a thick liquid. Molasses is more than 5,000 times thicker and heavier than water. The tank was overloaded and literally burst at the seams.

It unleashed a tsunami of molasses 35 feet high onto the streets of Boston. The molasses poured into the streets at 35 mph. It rolled over and crushed freight cars and lifted train engines off their tracks. It knocked the firehouse off its foundation. Buildings were smashed, electrical poles crashed, and live wires snapped and sparked.

The molasses rolled over people, horses, and dogs. Anything caught in the sticky substance was stuck like flies on flypaper. The brown liquid pulled them under, then filled their mouth and nose with molasses until they suffocated.

He yelled into the phone, "Send all available rescue vehicles and personnel immediately. There's a wave of molasses coming down Commercial Street!" McManus wasn't kidding.

There were 21 people who died in the flood and another 150 people who were injured by crashing buildings and floating debris. Besides the terrible human toll, there were many horses killed and buildings completely destroyed. In today's money, it would be more than $100 million in damages.

Once the police and firefighters had rescued as many people as they could, they began to clean up of the area. It was miserable. The sticky molasses started to harden and petrify like a city turned into molasses candy. They finally learned that salt water from the ocean would dissolve the molasses better than fresh water. With everyone working, it still took 80,000 man-hours to clean up the streets of Boston.

It goes down in history as one of the strangest and stickiest disasters in the world, but it is also a disaster that led to regular inspection of production plants and new safety regulations to protect the public.

DOOR TO HELL

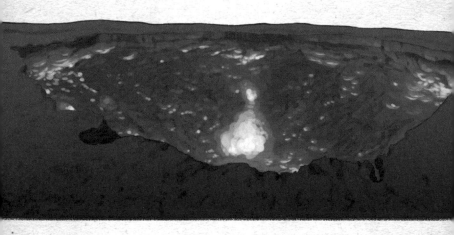

They call it the *Door to Hell*, and that's exactly what it looks like. It is a huge fiery crater the size of a football field in the middle of the desert in Turkmenistan, and it's been on fire for more than 45 years.

What caused the hole, and when did it start burning? Apparently in 1971, a group of Soviet scientists went to the desert looking for oil and natural gas reserves. They set up a drilling rig and began work in what they believed was a promising location. Unfortunately, the Soviets didn't realize they

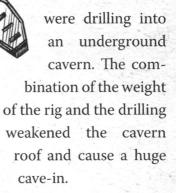

were drilling into an underground cavern. The combination of the weight of the rig and the drilling weakened the cavern roof and cause a huge cave-in.

Rocks, sand, and drilling equipment disappeared into a hole nearly 100 feet deep. And out of the ground burst a large amount of natural gas. Natural gas is not poisonous but contains a large amount of methane, and methane is highly flammable. Air that contains just 5% methane gas can explode.

The Soviet scientists' solution was to set the crater on fire. It is a standard procedure at many gas-drilling fields. When there is an excess of natural gas that is not able to be processed, the drillers set it on fire in a process called *flaring*. Usually the gas safely burns off in a few hours and it reduces the risk of unwanted explosions.

But the Soviet scientists set the fire without ever learning the amount of gas that was in the crater and the surrounding underground tunnels. The fire they set in 1971 has been continuously burning for more than 45 years. The result is disastrous. Millions of cubic feet of natural gas that could be used for energy is simply burned and released into the atmosphere. Putting out the fire could stop the waste and pollution, but the government of Turkmenistan does not have the scientific or financial resources to tackle the problem.

So the Door to Hell remains open, burning day and night. It's a man-made disaster that scientists are still trying to fix.

INTO THE PIT

Why would anybody want to climb into a pit of burning natural gas? To see if there is life in the pit, of course!

Only crazy people and scientists would think about looking for signs of life inside the Door to Hell. George Kourounis is both. The explorer teamed up with *National Geographic* to take a trip down into the crater to get sam-

~continues on page 95~

INTO THE PIT

~continued from page 94~

ples of rocks and see if there could be any microbes that could live in temperatures of 1,000 degrees centigrade (1,832 Fahrenheit).

In November of 2013, Kourounis put on a heat reflective suit and breathing apparatus and used Kevlar ropes to go into the burning pit. A crew from *National Geographic* filmed his descent and recorded him collecting rocks from the bottom of the crater.

Kourounis described it as being in a coliseum of fire. The walls of the crater are covered with thousands of small fires. He could see clearly without problems of smoke because the methane burns very clean.

Once the rocks were examined in the lab, Kourounis and his team were excited to find that there were indeed microbes living on the rocks in the methane-rich environment. This discovery proves that there could be microbial life on planets that have similar atmospheres. It is information scientists will use as they investigate planets outside of Earth's solar system.

FUKUSHIMA DISASTER

Children and teachers were doing all the normal things students do on a Friday afternoon in Sendai, Japan. They were working on math problems, finishing reports, and studying their history. But at 2:46 p.m. on March 11, 2011, buzzers started going off in offices, on cell phones, and in schools.

Teachers and children knew what to do. They had all practiced earthquake drills. They crawled under desks, covered their heads, and waited for the shaking to begin. And it came.

Walls shook and books flew off shelves. Glass beakers and test tubes smashed to the ground, and science rooms were covered in glass. Adults working in office buildings watched as shelves shook off the walls, leaving the contents broken on the floor. The earthquake was so strong that it felt like the Earth had turned into the ocean and the ground was moving in waves. Then, the shaking stopped.

> Hundreds of lives had been saved by Japan's early warning system. People breathed a sigh of relief. Surely the worst was over.

Teachers led students out of the school building into the open, away from collapsing walls. Adults poured out of damaged buildings into the open air. Hundreds of lives had been saved by Japan's early warning system. People breathed a sigh of relief. Surely the worst was over.

But what they didn't know was they had just survived one of the strongest earthquakes in modern history. It was a magnitude 9 on the Richter scale, with 10 being the highest level on the scale. The epicenter of the earthquake on the seafloor was 45 miles out in the ocean. The earthquake was so strong it pushed up a section of sea floor 66 feet and dropped the coastline by 2 feet. This action, combined with the earthquake, caused a huge tsunami with 30-foot waves to crash into the northeast coast of Japan.

Small fishing villages disappeared under the huge waves, and entire towns were immediately destroyed. People scrambled to the top floors of buildings and even on the rooftops only to have the entire building wash away. The few survivors told stories of clinging to floating logs or pieces of boats and watching as dead bodies floated past them.  More than 13,000 people were killed by the walls of water, and another 6,000 were injured.

But even that was not the end of the destruction, because the tsunami also flooded an area called the Fukushima Daini Nuclear Power Plant, destroying the emergency generators of the nuclear plant. Without the emergency generators, the reactors overheated and caused three nuclear meltdowns that released radioactive material into the air.

So, all in one day, the people of Japan suffered one of the world's strongest earthquakes, a killer tsunami, and a nuclear meltdown. March 11,

March 11, 2011 will go down in history as a day of total disaster.

2011 will go down in history as a day of total disaster.

Because of the threat of radiation poisoning and the risk of death from cancer, Japanese officials evacuated all the people living in a 12.5-mile radius around the nuclear plant. More than 150,000 people had to be removed from the area.

The devastation to Japan was unbelievable. The earthquake and tsunami had destroyed more than 1 million buildings and the nuclear disaster had made thousands more people homeless. In one day, Japan was suddenly faced with 470,000 people who needed homes, food, and clothing.

Help began pouring in from around the world. Donations and relief workers came from 116 different countries. It was a disaster so large that it would take thousands of workers and billions of dollars to help Japan clean up the debris. Scientists estimate that the Pacific Ocean still contains more than 1 million tons of debris and trash from the disaster.

GHOST SHIPS

Nearly 4 years after the disaster, parts of a Japanese fishing ship washed up on the coast of Oregon. The cargo of the ship contained yellowtail jack fish, a type of fish caught off the coast of Japan—and some of the fish were still alive. In the past few years, more than 26 Japanese ships have washed up on the West Coast of America. All of them are from the 2011 tsunami.

Ghost ships—intact ships with no living crews—have been found floating in the Pacific Ocean as a result of the tsunami. One such ship had to be sunk by the U.S. Coast Guard. You can see pictures of it at https://www.theguardian.com/world/gallery/2012/apr/06/tsunami-ghost-ship-us-coast-guard.

Science Lab

FOG IT UP

You can see how fog is made with this simple experiment. Don't worry—there's no acid involved, so it won't be a killer fog.

MATERIALS

- » Glass jar
- » Strainer
- » Water
- » Ice cubes

First, fill up the jar with hot tap water. Let it stand for 2 minutes. Pour out all but one inch of water. Then, put four ice cubes in the strainer. Place the strainer over the mouth of the jar. Watch to see the fog form.

The cold air from the ice cubes collides with the warm air in the glass jar and causes the water in the air to condense and form fog.

When you see fog in nature, it is a collection of water droplets just like in your experiment. Fog is basically a type of low-hanging cloud. It causes problems by reducing the visibility for drivers and airplane pilots.

FOGGY DAYS

The foggiest place in the world is the Grand Banks off the island of Newfoundland with 206 days of fog every year.

Science Lab

THE DENSITY DILEMMA

Why was the molasses spill so devastating? Because molasses is a dense liquid and that density gave it more power to destroy buildings.

Density is the amount of matter packed into a space. If you take two balloons and fill one with water and the other with air, which will weigh more? The water balloon, of course. We know water has more density, or matter packed into the same space, than air does. Liquids have different densities, too.

Try this experiment to see how density can affect liquids.

MATERIALS

- » 3 toothpicks
- » 3 grapes
- » Olive oil
- » Water
- » Molasses
- » Three small cups
- » Measuring cups
- » Clear glass jar with lid

Separately pour 1/2 cup of each liquid into the small cups, so that you will have one cup that contains olive oil, one cup that contains water, and one cup that contains molasses.

Poke one toothpick into each grape, so that the toothpick sticks out of the grape like a handle. Then push one grape into each type of liquid so that the grape is totally submerged. Wait a few seconds and now try to pull the grape back out. What happens? Is it easier to pull the grape out of oil or water? What about molasses or water? What if you had to pull a person out of each liquid? How hard would it be?

Now, you are going to "stack" the different liquids in the jar. You will need to measure 1/2 cup of molasses and pour it into the jar. Next, add 1/2 cup water. Pour it in on top of the molasses. Let it settle and wait a few minutes. Then, pour in 1/2 cup of oil. Let the jar stand for 3 or 4 minutes. What happens to the liquids?

They separate into layers because their densities are different. Put the lid on the jar and shake it up. What happens to the liquids? Let it sit again and watch them separate. How do you think this affected the people and buildings involved in the Great Molasses Disaster?

AVALANCHE KING

The mountain looks peaceful covered in a blanket of white show. Tops of trees poke through the white, and cold blue skies glow overhead. It looks like the perfect day to start an avalanche.

The rangers carefully select the spot on the mountain. They have years of training and can spot the small cracks in the ice and snow that indicate an avalanche might happen. Their objective is to start the avalanche on purpose. If they control when the snow and ice crash down the mountain, they can keep people out of the way. They can also reduce the amount of damage to forests and homes by starting small frequent avalanches instead of one huge destructive avalanche.

All it takes is training and a good supply of explosives. Avalanche hunters are trained by the U.S. Forest Service and usually ski into an area to examine its safety. They may plant explosives and then blow them up remotely, or sometimes they are able to use a pneumatic gun to actually shoot the snow and cause the avalanche from a distance.

The practice of starting controlled avalanches was pioneered by forester Montgomery Meigs Atwater. As a forest ranger in the 1940s, he established the first avalanche research center in the Western Hemisphere. He had to do a lot of talking to convince the U.S. Forest Service that blowing up a mountain of snow would actually be a good thing. But he proved it over and over again by making the mountains in his area avalanche free.

He was so good at hunting and destroying avalanches that he was selected to serve as the director of avalanche control for the 1960 Winter Olympics. Under Atwater's watch, there was not a single avalanche to spoil the Olympic games. No avalanche would fall while the Avalanche King was on guard.

Montgomery Meigs Atwater

Today, the Forest Service and specially trained volunteers still scour the mountains looking for signs of avalanches. By setting off controlled avalanches, they save hundreds of thousands of dollars in damage and many lives.

HURRICANE HUNTERS

Dark storm clouds gather over the Atlantic Ocean. The winds swirl, and rain feels heavy in the air. It's the time when most people think about hunkering down inside and hiding from the weather. But for the aircrew of the 53rd Weather Reconnaissance Squadron, it's time to suit up and scramble for the airplane. They are the Hurricane Hunters, and it's their job to fly into

oncoming storms to collect data and information that will help meteorologists make accurate weather predictions.

Each hurricane team consists of five people. The pilot and copilot are charged with keeping the plane and crew safe and flying the mission. The navigator watches the radar and tracks the plane's position relative to the storm. The flight meteorologist monitors all the atmospheric data and helps guide the aircraft to the hurricane center. The weather reconnaissance loadmaster makes sure all meteorological equipment is working and recording data.

[Flying into a hurricane or tropical storm is not an easy task and takes skilled pilots and a team who can problem solve.]

Flying into a hurricane or tropical storm is not an easy task and takes skilled pilots and a team who can problem solve. Hurricane crews have flown in storms that have winds that are higher than 180 mph. When flying through the hurricane eyewall, there can be huge wind updrafts and downdrafts that make the plane rise and fall quickly. Equipment in the plane can be thrown around and the crew has to watch out.

The sudden shifts in the altitude of the plane feel like going up and down on a superfast rollercoaster and actually exert gravitational pull on the pilots and their team. The G-meter can go as high as +5 Gs or as low as -3Gs. Upward Gs drive the blood down to the feet and downward Gs push blood to the head and eyes. Higher than 5Gs will cause the typical human to lose consciousness.

Once the plane reaches the eye of the storm, the crew releases a special sensor called a drop-sonde. The drop-sonde is attached to a special para-chute, and as it falls, the instru-ment records the temperature, pres-sure, wind speed, and humidity of

Information that meteorologists get from the Hurricane Hunter planes greatly increases the accuracy of storm predictions. With the help of the Hurricane Hunters, weather reports are 30% more accurate.

the atmosphere. The data is transmitted back to the aircraft, and meteorologists use the information to make accurate storm predictions.

Information that meteorologists get from the Hurricane Hunter planes greatly increases the accuracy of storm predictions. With the help of the Hurricane Hunters, weather reports are 30% more accurate. This helps save lives because officials know where major storms are going to hit, and they can issue accurate warnings for people to evacuate. The Hurricane Hunters risk their own lives to save the lives of others.

WHAT'S IN A (HURRICANE) NAME?

Have you ever wondered why hurricanes sport common (and uncommon) names? Hurricanes and tropical storms have been given human names for at least 100 years, primarily because it's easier for people to remember names than numbers. Names make people more interested in the storms *and* more likely to be prepared for when storms head their way. The World Meteorological Society (WMO) keeps six lists of possible hurricane names, rotating the lists every six years (so 2016's list will be used again in 2022) for storms that occur in the Caribbean Sea, the Gulf of Mexico, and the North Atlantic. The lists began with using just female names, introducing male names in 1979. And the lists do change occasionally—when a particularly deadly or costly storm comes along, its name is retired from the list and a new name is chosen to replace it. Katrina (2005), Sandy (2012), and Haiyan (2013) are just a few of the names removed in recent years due to the severity of their storm. It's not just the North American storms that get names either— other countries have other naming systems to keep their tropical storms and hurricanes straight.

SMOKE JUMPERS

When the forest catches on fire, most people run the other direction, but not smoke-jumpers. They put on fireproof parachutes and jump out of an airplane, trying to land as close to the fire as possible. Some people think they are crazy, but these disaster workers are the first people who are called when a fire is spotted. Their job is to put the fire out before it grows.

They are an elite team of firefighters employed by the U.S. Forest Service. To qualify for this job, they have to be in top physical shape and able to run while wearing 40-pounds worth of firefighting gear and carrying a 110-pound pack. They need to know first aid, survival skills, and orienteering. They are often dropped in remote locations hundreds of miles from any ranger station or town. If they don't have the skills to survive, they won't make it out of the forest fire alive.

It's a terribly dangerous job. Jumping out of a plane into a fire isn't like recreational skydiving. The heat of the fires causes updrafts and makes it difficult to steer the parachute. Landing is treacherous. If they are lucky, the smokejumpers land in a clearing with both feet on the ground. The impact is so hard that it has been known to break a person's leg. If they are unlucky, their parachute can get caught in a tree. Then they have to cut themselves out of their chute and climb down the tree. And they need to do it before the tree catches on fire.

Smokejumper teams are small, with usually no more than 20 people on a team. Currently, there are around 500 qualified smokejumpers in the United States. Their objective is to be flexible and fast-moving in order to stop a blaze before it can turn into a massive forest fire. They are stationed in states with large amounts of forests, such as California, Washington, and Montana, but they can be called to fight a fire anywhere in the U.S. and have even been sent overseas to help with fires in other countries.

> Jumping out of a plane into a fire isn't like recreational skydiving. The heat of the fires causes updrafts and makes it difficult to steer the parachute.

The idea of using airplanes to help with firefighting has been around almost since the invention of the flying machine. The U.S. Forest Service started using planes as early as 1917 to help spot fires in remote timber. In the 1920s, they experimented with different ways to fight fire from the air. They tried filling 8-gallon wooden beer kegs with water

Today's Smokejumper equipment

and dropping the kegs on the fires. They also tried dropping 5-gallon tin cans of water and paper bags filled with foam. It had limited success with putting out fires, but it did lead to the practice of parachuting supplies in to firefighters in remote areas.

It was in 1939 that a team of young men began training for the new job of smokejumper, and by June of 1940 the first official team of six jumpers went to work putting out nine fires that summer. By 1958, there were 325 certified smokejumpers extinguishing fires. During the next six decades, nearly 6,000 men and women served as elite firefighters jumping from the sky into the fire. Their ability to contain small fires and prevent infernos has saved millions of acres of old growth forest and millions of taxpayer dollars.

SUPER SEAMSTRESS

Not only do smokejumpers have to be tough and brave, but they also have to know how to run a sewing machine. Smokejumpers have to sew their own jumpsuits, harnesses, and gear bags. Because there are less than 500 smokejumpers in the whole nation, it is not cost effective for manufacturers to make commercial suits. And, because there aren't any supply stores that carry what they need, the smokejumpers have to sew their own.

New recruits don't have to worry if they don't know how to sew—a veteran will give them lessons. The smokejumpers also design their own patterns and make adjustments as new materials are available.

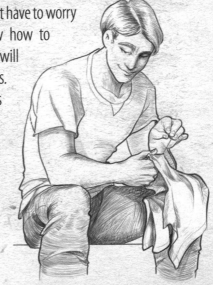

INTO THE VOLCANO

S am Cossman has done something very few humans have ever tried. He stood on the edge of a sea of volcanic lava and lived to tell the story. He also got some amazing video.

Cossman calls himself a modern explorer and he uses technology to help him go to places where humans have not been able to safely visit. In 2015, he made his second trip inside the Marum Crater in the South Pacific. He put on a custom-made flame retardant suit and walked to the edge of an active volcano. The heat of the lava was so intense it melted his facemask and incinerated the camera-carrying drones he had flying above.

In order to get down to the lava, Cossman had to use fireproof climbing gear to repel 1,200 feet into the caldera of the volcano. He had to watch out for falling boulders, acid rain, and flying chunks of molten rock. One slip, and he would have fallen to his death. But Cossman made it, even if all of his drones didn't.

Despite the loss of some of the camera drones, Cossman and his team were able to film enough of the crater that they are making a 3-D map of the interior of the volcano. The team also took samples of lava, rocks, and volcanic gasses. These samples are being studied by scientists to learn more about the interior regions of the Earth. They are also studying how microbial life could exist and grow in such an extreme environment.

In order to get down to the lava, Cossman had to use fireproof climbing gear to repel 1,200 feet into the caldera of the volcano.

ON THE EDGE OF YOUR VOLCANO

You can watch Sam Cossman's amazing video at http://video.nationalgeographic.com/video/short-film-show case/mind-blowing-video-from-volcanos-edge.

ROBOT EXPLORER

Going inside a volcano is incredibly dangerous for humans. Not only can burning lava kill humans, but there also are poisonous gases and high heat. It makes learning about the inside of the Earth really difficult.

But Carolyn Parcheta, a NASA scientist, came up with a solution. She has developed a robot that can crawl into volcanic crevices and explore volcanic vents. Called *VolcanoBots*, these two-wheeled little robots can climb down the volcano walls, won't be affected by poisonous gas, and can withstand much higher temperatures than any human.

If the VolcanoBots prove successful in exploring Earth's volcanoes, their next assignment may be a trip to outer space to explore the volcanoes on other planets.

Science Lab

MEASURE WIND SPEED

 Measuring wind speed is one way that forecasters predict oncoming storms. You can build a model of an anemometer—the tool used for measuring wind speed.

MATERIALS

» 5 small paper cups	» Empty water bottle
» Hole punch	» Sand
» Scissors	» Stopwatch
» 3 thin wooden dowel sticks	» Duct tape

Punch a hole in the side of four paper cups (make sure to lay your cups facing in the same direction before picking the side on which to punch the hole). On the fifth cup, punch four holes evenly spaced around the rim. This cup will be used as the center of your anemometer.

Take two of the wooden dowels and slide them through the holes of the center cup. The dowels should form a cross in the center.

Place one cup on the end of each arm of the dowel rod cross. Secure the ends of the dowel rods with tape.

Take the third dowel rod and make a hole in the bottom of the center cup. Push the dowel up until it meets the cross section of the two dowel arms. Then tape all of this together. This will make the rotation axis for the anemometer.

Pour at least 2 inches of sand into the bottle to give it anchor weight.

Then place the center dowel into the bottle. Keep the stick above the sand so it will move in the wind.

Now you can calibrate your anemometer for wind speed.

Take the anemometer outside and place it on the ground so that the cups can catch the breeze. Use the stopwatch to see how many complete turns your anemometer makes in one minute. Repeat this four more times, and then average your totals together. This is the wind speed for today. To see how the wind speed changes, do the same experiment for a week. Does the wind speed stay the same each day? Do windy days bring storms or fair weather? Compare your observations with the daily weather reports.

Science Lab

BUILD A VOLCANO

You know you want to do it! So come on—get your hands dirty and build an exploding volcano. Of course, you can't get hot lava all over Mom's kitchen, so you will need to substitute baking soda and vinegar, but it will erupt out of a mountaintop just like Vesuvius!

MATERIALS

- » 6 cup flour
- » 2 cups salt
- » 4 tablespoons cooking oil
- » 2 cups warm water
- » Large mixing bowl
- » Empty 2-liter bottle
- » Baking pan
- » Funnel and water pitcher (optional)
- » Red food coloring
- » Liquid dish soap
- » Stirring stick
- » Baking soda
- » Vinegar
- » Water

In the mixing bowl, combine the flour, salt, cooking oil, and warm water to make a playdough-like substance. You will use this to create the outer part of the volcano.

Stand the bottle in the center of the cooking pan and mold the dough around the bottle in the shape of a volcanic mountain. Make sure to leave the mouth of the bottle clear.

Once you have finished your mountain, fill the bottle with warm water, almost to the top. Leave at least 2 inches of air space at the top of the bottle. It may be easier to do this using the funnel and a pitcher of warm water.

Add a few drops of food coloring to the bottle and then put in 10 drops of liquid soap. Stir this together in the bottle.

Add 2 heaping tablespoons of baking soda to the bottle and stir.

Now get ready for your volcanic explosion— grab that vinegar and slowly pour it into the top of your volcano. It will fizz and spew lava! But fortunately, it won't melt the kitchen or catch your house on fire!

BIBLIOGRAPHY

BOOKS

Bechtel, S., & Samaras, T. (2009). *Tornado hunter: Getting inside the most violent storms on Earth.* Washington, DC: National Geographic.

Haerens, M., & Zott, L. (Ed.). (2013). *Natural disasters (Opposing viewpoints).* Detroit, MI: Greenhaven Press.

Hayes, W. (2011). *Popular mechanics—What went wrong: Investigating the worst man-made and natural disasters.* New York, NY: Hearst.

Klingaman, W. K., & Klingaman, N. P. (2013). *The year without summer: 1816 and the volcano that darkened the world and changed history.* New York, NY: St. Martin's Press.

Ramos, J. A., & Smith, J. (2015). *Smokejumper: A memoir by one of America's most select airborne firefighters.* New York, NY: William Morrow.

Sandlin, L. (2013). *Storm kings: The untold story of America's first tornado chasers.* New York, NY: Pantheon Books.

Svensen, H. (2012). *The end is nigh: A history of natural disasters.* London, England: Reaktion Books.

Walker, S. M. (2011). *Blizzard of glass: The Halifax Explosion of 1917.* New York, NY: Henry Holt and Co.

Withington, J. (2010). *Disaster! A history of earthquakes, floods, plagues, and other catastrophes.* New York, NY: Skyhorse Publishing.

WEBSITES

Bell, T. E., & Phillips, T. (2008). A super solar flare. *NASA Science News.* Retrieved from http://science.nasa.gov/science-news/science-at-nasa/2008/06may_carringtonflare

Bjornsson, E. (2013). How to make an anemometer. *Education.com.* Retrieved from http://www.education.com/science-fair/article/make-anemometer

Bressan, D. (2015). The Tunguska Event: Still a mystery after 107 years. *Forbes.* Retrieved from http://www.forbes.com/sites/davidbressan/2015/06/30/the-tunguska-event-still-a-mystery-after-107-years/#638919f91e98

Brown, D. W. (2015). 10 things you didn't know about smokejumpers. *Mental Floss.* Retrieved from http://mentalfloss.com/article/67000/10-things-you-didnt-know-about-smokejumpers

Burnham-on-Sea.com. (n.d.). *1607 flood in the Bristol Channel—Was it a UK tsunami?* Retrieved from http://www.burnham-on-sea.com/1607-flood.shtml

Charlton, C. (2015). See you in hell: Explorer becomes the first person to descend into Turkmenistan's 1,000C pit of fire which has not stopped burning since 1971. *DailyMail.com*. Retrieved from http://www.dailymail.co.uk/news/article-3070043/See-Hell-Explorer-person-descend-Turkmenistan-s-1-000C-pit-fire-not-stopped-burning-1971.html

Denmark, B. (2014). The Great Smog of '52: Environmental disasters in history. *Vision learning*. Retrieved from http://www.vision learning.com/blog/2014/12/03/great-smog-52-environmental-disasters-history

Devastating Disasters. (2016). *Aleppo earthquake–Syria–1138 AD*. Retrieved from http://devastatingdisasters.com/aleppo-earthquake-syria-1138-ad

EyeWitness to History. (1999). *The destruction of Pompeii, 79 AD*. Retrieved from http://www.eyewitnesstohistory.com/pompeii.htm

Galvin, J. (2007). Tri-State Tornado: Missouri, Illinois, Indiana, March 1925. *Popular Mechanics*. Retrieved from http://www.popular mechanics.com/science/environment/a1965/4219866

Geiling, N. (2014). This hellish desert pit has been on fire for more than 40 years. *Smithsonian Magazine*.

Retrieved from http://www.smithsonianmag.
com/travel/giant-hole-ground-has-been-fire-
more-40-years-180951247

Gillis, D. (2015). The forgotten fire. *Damn Interesting*.
Retrieved from https://www.damninteresting.
com/the-forgotten-fire

Havel, G. (2007). Remembering the Great Peshtigo
Fire of 1871. *Fire Engineering*. http://www.fire
engineering.com/articles/2007/10/remember
ing-the-great-peshtigo-fire-of-1871.html

Hays, J. (2012). Great tsunami of 2004 in Thailand.
Facts and Details. Retrieved from http://factsand
details.com/asian/cat63/sub411/item2543.
html

Hogenboom, M. (2016). In Siberia in 1908, a huge
explosion came out of nowhere. *BBC Earth*.
Retrieved from http://www.bbc.com/earth/
story/20160706-in-siberia-in-1908-a-huge-
explosion-came-out-of-nowhere

Hottensen, C. (2015). Survivors remember Tri-State
Tornado 90 years later. *The Southern Illinoisan*.
Retrieved from http://thesouthern.com/news/
local/surivors-remember-tri-state-tornado-
years-later/article_aaa494e1-8cce-5d12-bd92-
b8638fe33056.html

Hurricane Hunters Association. (n.d.) *The mission of the hurricane hunters*. Retrieved from http://www.hurricanehunters.com/mission.html

Jabr, F. (2013). The science of The Great Molasses Flood. *Scientific American*. Retrieved from http://www.scientificamerican.com/article/molasses-flood-physics-science

Jacobson, R. (2014). The day that changed tsunami science. *PBS News Hour*. Retrieved from http://www.pbs.org/newshour/updates/tsunami-changed-science

Kayzar, T. (n.d.). *The Lake Nyos disaster*. Retrieved from http://www.geo.arizona.edu/geo5xx/geos577/projects/kayzar/html/lake_nyos_disaster.html

Klein, C. (2012a). The killer fog that blanketed London. *History.com*. Retrieved from http://www.history.com/news/the-killer-fog-that-blanketed-london-60-years-ago

Klein, C. (2012b). A perfect solar superstorm: The 1859 Carrington Event. *History.com*. Retrieved from http://www.history.com/news/a-perfect-solar-superstorm-the-1859-carrington-event

Klein, C. (2014). The London beer flood. *History. com*. Retrieved from http://www.history.com/news/the-london-beer-flood-200-years-ago

Krajick, K. (2003). Defusing Africa's killer lakes. *Smithsonian Magazine*. Retrieved from http://www.smithsonianmag.com/science-nature/defusing-africas-killer-lakes-88765263/?no-ist=&page=5

Landau, E. (2015). NASA robot plunges into volcano to explore fissure. *NASA Technology*. Retrieved from http://www.nasa.gov/jpl/nasa-robot-plunges-into-volcano-to-explore-fissure

Live Science. (2009). *12 twisted tornado facts*. Retrieved from http://www.livescience.com/3589-12-twisted-tornado-facts.html

Lyons, C. (2009). A sticky tragedy: The Boston molasses disaster. *History Today, 59*(1). Retrieved from http://www.historytoday.com/chuck-lyons/sticky-tragedy-boston-molasses-disaster

Mersereau, D. (2016). 15 facts about 'The year without a summer.' *Mental Floss*. Retrieved from http://mentalfloss.com/article/73585/15-facts-about-year-without-summer

Miller, D. J. (1960). *Eyewitness accounts from survivors*. United States Geological Survey

Professional Paper 354-C. Retrieved from http://geology.com/records/biggest-tsunami.shtml#eyewitness

National Center for Atmospheric Research. (2016). *Mount Tambora and the year without summer.* Retrieved from http://scied.ucar.edu/shortcontent/mount-tambora-and-year-without-summer

National Geographic News. (2005). *The deadliest tsunami in history?* Retrieved from http://news.nationalgeographic.com/news/2004/12/1227_041226_tsunami.html

New Zealand Herald. (2005). *Tsunami stories: Beach 'angel' saves hundreds.* Retrieved from http://www.nzherald.co.nz/world/news/article.cfm?c_id=2&objectid=9005390

Nunez, C. (2014). Q & A: The first-ever expedition to Turkmenistan's "Door to Hell." *National Geographic.* Retrieved from http://news.nationalgeographic.com/news/energy/2014/07/140716-door-to-hell-darvaza-crater-george-kourounis-expedition

Oskin, B. (2015). Japan earthquake & tsunami of 2011: Facts and information. *LiveScience.* Retrieved from http://www.livescience.com/

39110-japan-2011-earthquake-tsunami-facts.
html

Pernin, P. (1971). The Great Peshtigo Fire: An eye-witness account. *Wisconsin Magazine of History*, *54*, 246–272. Retrieved from http://digicoll.library.wisc.edu/WIReader/WER2002-0.html

Rice, D. (2016). 200 years ago, we endured 'a year without a summer.' *USA Today*. Retrieved from http://www.usatoday.com/story/weather/2016/05/26/year-without-a-summer-1816-mount-tambora/84855694

Rogers, S. A. (n.d.). Ancient engineering fail: 12 historic structural disasters. *Web Urbanist*. Retrieved from http://weburbanist.com/2014/04/16/ancient-engineering-fail-12-historic-structural-disasters

Schuppe, J. (2015.) Explorer uses drones to peer inside a volcano. *NBC News*. Retrieved from http://www.nbcnews.com/news/us-news/explorer-uses-drones-peer-inside-volcano-n314151

Shawn. (2013). *March 18, 1925—The Tri-State Tornado* [Weblog post]. Retrieved from https://stormstalker.wordpress.com/2013/06/10/tri-state-tornado

Stewart, D. (2006). Resurrecting Pompeii. *Smithsonian Magazine.* Retrieved from http://www.smithsonianmag.com/history/resurrecting-pompeii-109163501/?no-ist%2F=&page=4

The Telegraph. (2016). *Hurricane names—How are they decided?* Retrieved from http://www.telegraph.co.uk/news/0/hurricane-names---how-are-they-decided

Trex, E. (2011). Boston's Great Molasses Flood of 1919. *Mental Floss.* Retrieved from http://mentalfloss.com/article/27366/bostons-great-molasses-flood-1919

University of Rhode Island. (n.d.). *Hurricane hunters.* Retrieved from http://www.hurricanescience.org/science/observation/aircraftrecon/hurricanehunters

U.S. Forest Service. (2008). *National smokejumper training guide–USFS-2008.* Retrieved from http://www.fs.fed.us/fire/aviation/av_library/sj_guide/02_history_of_smokejumping.pdf

Wikipedia. (n.d.). *Aleppo earthquake.* Retrieved from https://en.wikipedia.org/wiki/1138_Aleppo_earthquake

Wikipedia. (n.d.). *Fidenae.* Retrieved from https://en.wikipedia.org/wiki/Fidenae

Wikipedia. (n.d.). *Lists of earthquakes*. Retrieved from https://en.wikipedia.org/wiki/Lists_of_earthquakes

Worrall, S. (2015). What it's like to plunge into the heart of a forest fire. *National Geographic*. Retrieved from http://news.nationalgeographic.com/2015/07/150729-fire-smokejumpers-forestry-yarnell-fire-ngbooktalk

YouTube. (2009). *Angel of the beach* [Video file]. Retrieved from https://www.youtube.com/watch?v=6C3CJX1-d_8&index=2&list=RD6C3CJX1-d_8

Zimmerman-Wall, S. (2009). Taming the white tiger. *Utah Adventure Journal*. Retrieved from http://utahadvjournal.com/index.php/taming-the-white-tiger

ABOUT THE AUTHOR

Stephanie Bearce is a writer, teacher, and science nerd. She likes teaching kids how to blow up toothpaste and dissect worms. She also loves collecting rocks and keeps a huge collection of fossilized bones in her basement. When she is not exploding experiments in her kitchen or researching strange science facts in the library, Stephanie likes to explore catacombs and museums with her husband, Darrell.

MORE TWISTED TRUE TALES FROM SCIENCE

Twisted True Tales From Science: Explosive Experiments

ISBN: 978-1-61821-576-5

Two thousand years ago, Chinese scientists were looking for a medicine that would make them live forever. Instead, they blew up their lab and discovered gunpowder. Alfred Nobel blew up his laboratory twice before he discovered the formula for dynamite. Learn about the Apollo 13 and Challenger explosions and the strange space explosions caused by top secret Starfish Prime. These stories may sound twisted, but they're all true tales from science!

MORE TWISTED TRUE TALES FROM SCIENCE

Twisted True Tales From Science: Insane Inventors

978-1-61821-570-3

Nikola Tesla was crazy smart. He invented the idea for cell phones in 1893, discovered alternating current, and invented a death ray gun. Of course, he also talked to pigeons, ate only boiled food, and was scared of women who wore jewelry. He was an insane inventor. So was Henry Cavendish, who discovered hydrogen, calculated the density of the Earth, and was so scared of people that he had to write notes to communicate. Sir Isaac Newton discovered the laws of gravity, believed in magic, and thought he could make a potion to create gold. These stories may sound twisted, but they're all true tales from science!

MORE TWISTED TRUE TALES FROM SCIENCE

Twisted True Tales From Science: Medical Mayhem
978-1-61821-572-7

Ground-up mummy bones, leeches sucking human blood, and a breakfast of dried mouse paste. It sounds like a horror movie, but those were actual medicines prescribed by early doctors. Medical students studied anatomy on bodies stolen from graves and had to operate on people while they were awake. Learn about the medicines that came from poison and doctors who experimented on themselves and their families. It's a twisted tale of medical mayhem, but it's all true!